THE

ENCHANTED

MIND

A New Vision For
Inner Space & Body

by

Richard A. Zarro

TRANS TECH PUB., CO.
Post Office Box 489
Woodstock, NY 12498

The author gratefully acknowledges the following sources for permission to reprint brief passages:

Peak Performance: Mental Training Techniques of the World's Greatest Athletes by Charles A. Garfield with Hal Zina Bennett, © 1984 by Charles A. Garfield, reprinted by permission of Jeremy P. Tarcher, Inc., Los Angeles. Excerpts from *The I Ching Workbook* by R.L. Wing. Copyright © 1979 by Immedia, Reprinted by permission of Doubleday, a division of Bantam, Doubleday, Dell Publishing Group, Inc. "Research Affirms Power of Positive Thinking" by Daniel Goleman, *New York Times,* February 3, 1987, © 1987 by The New York Times Company. Reprinted by permission. "Body and Soul" by David Gelman with Mary Hager, *Newsweek,* November 7, 1988, © 1988 *Newsweek. Mysticism and the New Physics* by Michael Talbot, © 1980 by Michael Talbot. From *Beyond the Quantum* by Michael Talbot. Copyright © 1986 by Michael Talbot. Reprinted with permission of Macmillan Publishing Company. Peak Press: an excerpt from *Who Gets Sick: Thinking and Health,* by Blair Justice, © 1987 by Blair Justice. Reprinted by permission of author and Peak Press.

Special Editorial Note: Some material in this book was extracted from chapters 3 and 4 of *Changing Your Destiny: Dynamic New Astrological and Visualization Tools to Shape Your Future,* written by Mary Orser and Richard A. Zarro in 1989. Originally published by Harper & Row, it has been translated into several other languages.

Senior Editor: Gail Goodman
Cover Design: Lori Stephens
Photo Credit (Back Cover): Bonnie Edwards Photography,
  White Plains, New York

Library of Congress Cataloging-in-Publication Data, etc.

Zarro, Richard A.
        The Enchanted Mind
        Includes bibliography

DEDICATION

To the late Michael Talbot, inspiring author and friend, and to all my students and associates who allow me the privilege of fulfilling my profound need to serve the planet.

ACKNOWLEDGMENTS
(in alphabetical order)

David Balding, president of Metamorphous Press, for his constant advice and creating a conduit for my work. **Matthew J. Barbis** for his copyreading, ideas, and growing friendship. **Joe Brunetto** for his copyreading of the manuscript and our deepening friendship. **Dr. Marv Forrest** for *suggesting* I write the book and enriching my life with his friendship and loyalty. **Gail Goodman** for her brilliant insights, quality editing, and emotional support, without which this book would not have been written. **Dr. John Grinder** whose influence in my life continues to grow, enriching me always. Special thanks for his co-development of Neuro-Linguistic Programming (N.L.P.), which has revolutionized modern thinking. **Pat Koenig**, R.N., R.H., C.I., for *insisting* I write the book, her loyalty and faith in me, and her vision and creation of P.A.T.S. CARE, bringing the benefits of Holographic Hypnosis© into hospitals across the United States. **Yolanda McGrath** for her loving support and encouragement. **Dr. Ormond McGill** for his belief in my work, his gentle kindness, and flattering introduction. **Mary Orser** for her friendship and co-authoring of *Changing Your Destiny*, which in great part inspired this book. **Ed Pym** for his fiscal advice, loving support, and encouragement. **Teri Roiger** for her typesetting, page designs, copyediting, and tireless rewrites. **Peter Schleim** for his insightful suggestions and focus. **Lori Stephens** for her creative vision and patience in designing the cover and handling the endless details involved in printing a book. **Steven J. Volpe**, R.H., for his administrative skills, dedication to F.T.I. and Holographic Hypnosis,© and his continual search for Truth.

CONTENTS

FOREWARD

by

Dr. Ormond McGill

Richard A. Zarro, R.H., C.I., is a Certified Hypnotherapist and scientist. He is the president of Futureshaping Technologies, Inc. The name of his company well describes his work in the field of Holographic Hypnosis, which presents a quantum leap into the creative use of the hypnosis of the future combined with the computer technology of today. Its advancement in the science of mind will take us into the 21st century.

Hardly more than ten years back hypnotherapy was little known as a profession. There were very few professional hypnotherapists. Today it has proved to be a major breakthrough for re-educating the mind for successful living. There are hundreds listed in the Yellow Pages of every phone book of every major city in the country — not only in the America but internationally. Schools both worldwide and in the U.S. provide expert certified training in the field. Conventions of hypnotherapists are held annually. Richard Zarro is one of the leaders, and in this book he shares his expertise with you to improve your life in every way. He is one of the first to develop a *standardized* method of hypnosis in the world.

We are currently living in what has become known as the "Computer Age." Computers are everywhere serving man's needs, and the technology of mind control advances in direct ratio to computer technology, for mind via the brain is a biocomputer ever there for you to operate for your personal use. Your personal biocomputer is greater than any electronic computer ever designed. The potentials of your biocomputer for success in the world are boundless.

You are what you think.

Mind and brain work as a unit. Mind is a process for producing thoughts, and thoughts are things. Thoughts are forms of energy. Your brain functions as a communication device that manifests your thoughts, via the wonderful mechanism that is your body, in three-dimensional space. But in actuality, space is not limited to three dimensions. It is multi-dimensional, and when you know how to fully use your potential of mind you can advance even beyond the physical world into realms of direct creativity. It is the way of the Universe, and man is a miniature of the Universe.

In this book, master hypnotherapist Richard Zarro will show you a revolutionary way to bring health, wealth, and success directly into your life. Read, study, and put into operation the powerful principles taught within these pages, and *the gateway of happiness will open wide for you!*

It's just the beginning . . .

Ormond McGill, Ph.D.
Palo Alto, California
1995

INTRODUCTION

We all heal ourselves.

Our bodies continually perform acts of healing. We take for granted the intelligence which silently and effortlessly heals a broken bone, or mends a cut on the skin. Modern scientific breakthroughs have blown open the doors to understanding the process of healing. With this understanding, we can develop some mastery of our state of health and maintain a sense of well-being that is greater than any we have ever experienced. New emerging research in science has unlocked the mystery of the mind-body connection. We can now learn to assume an active role in the process of healing.

At P.A.T.S. Care, Inc. *(Patients Augmenting Their Surgical Care)* we believe that a very important element is missing in medicine: the active participation of the patient. We need a new health care paradigm — one that challenges patients to see what they can do for themselves as a *complement* to their traditional medical treatments. Our program provides information and knowledge to patients about to undergo surgical procedures so they are able to participate in their own healing. It is our belief that such a support and information network greatly benefits patients and surgical caregivers.

I originally chose the profession of nursing because I wanted to meet patients' needs. In the '70's, medicine went high-tech and I found myself pulled into the role of "technical assistant." As the profession of nursing began to rapidly expand and diversify, I saw patients becoming less involved in their own healing process. The one *essential* ingredient to the entire health care system, the patient, was becoming *incidental.*

Simultaneously, the field of mind-body medicine was gaining more attention. One of its basic tenets is the patients should actively participate in healing. With this in mind, I began to research ways in which nurses, with their unique ability to care for patients, could bridge the gap between the latest scientific advances in medical care and mind-body medicine. How could nursing incorporate such diversity in a way that would be *complementary?*

My personal journey took me through a number of consciousness changing techniques, such as meditation, visualization, self-hypnosis, and guided imagery. I witnessed dramatic changes in myself and observed significant results occurring in other's lives as they learned and practiced these techniques. To incorporate these techniques into my nursing, I sought a more scientific model. Through a series of amazing coincidences, I met Richard Zarro, the author of this book. His dynamic teaching style caught my attention, and his breakthrough techniques earned my respect. He had accomplished the synthesis I was seeking and developed the only model with a *standardized* method of delivery. In addition, he had the gift of explaining his techniques in a clear, no-nonsense fashion that made sense to me as a medical professional, as well as my patients.

In his distinguished career, Richard Zarro has helped thousands to achieve personal excellence in their lives. He demystifies subjects that used to be considered esoteric: the mind-body connection, the effects of mental imagery on the body, and self-hypnosis. Best of all, he allows everyone to maintain their own spiritual belief system while helping them understand the nature of consciousness.

This book goes beyond wishful thinking about positive thinking. In it, you will learn how to increase your potential for meaningful self-expression and activate deep personal resources for whatever goal you choose.

As you read this book, you will begin to understand how choosing to participate in your healing will give you important tools to change all aspects of your life.

You are far more powerful than you realize!

Patricia Koenig, R.N., R.H., C.I.
P.A.T.S. Care Inc., Kingston, NY

PREFACE

THE TWO DOORS
An Ancient Fable

Once upon a time, in ancient China, there was an emperor. He had many wives who were guarded by the royal eunuchs while he entertained himself with gambling and public games. Unfortunately, one of the emperor's most trusted generals fell in love with one of his favorite wives, and ran away with her. Upon capture, they were returned to the court for punishment.

Although it was in his power to simply cut off their heads, the emperor decided to extract a unique punishment which would satisfy his need to show complete domain over all subjects, wives and generals included.

He brought all his subjects to the amphitheater and in the middle was placed the captured male lover. There were two doors in the rear of this theater and to all in attendance he announced, "I have put the general's fate in the hands of my wife, who has been his lover. Behind one door is a hungry tiger. Behind the other door is a beautiful unmarried maiden. One choice will bring him certain and painful death. The other will spare him and grant him a happy and long life, though with another woman. My wife knows what is behind each door. I put his life in her hands, and so his future is hers to decide."

With that, he turned to his beautiful, albeit pale, wife. He smiled at her distress.

The woman looked down at her fear-filled lover. On one hand, she could send him to death. On the other, she could send him to a fate which, while granting him bodily life, would subject her to emotional death.

The emperor then said, *"Dearest unfaithful wife, you may now choose."*

The beautiful wife pointed to the door on the left.

*

Did he find the beautiful maiden or the ravenous tiger?

The answer you just thought of is very important to you. It will give you an idea about how you move through life — with trust or distrust, optimism or pessimism. We will be discussing this later and give you the answer to the riddle.

PART ONE

THE
ENCHANTED
MIND

*

"What is believed becomes reality
and all possible pasts, presents, and futures are like
different channels on a television set."

MICHAEL TALBOT
Mysticism and the New Physics

THE POWER OF ATTENTION AND THE HOLOGRAPHIC MIND

The mind has been likened to a biocomputer. The very quality of your life depends on whether you are its master or slave. Your understanding of this tool is the key to shaping your future. Your mind is an amazing tool of unlimited potential.

In every generation, a small group of people have realized this profound potential. However, most of the population, including our own Western culture, has downplayed, or overtly denied the role of mind over matter. At best, it was a "philosophy" or unproved theory. It is now a proven, researched fact; no longer a theory. I will describe how awareness of the mind's vast powers has been resurfacing in many fields of knowledge, especially those relating to optimum health. I will discuss *what* the mind is capable of and give you simple techniques to make full use of its hidden potential. This allows you better control of your body, your health, your well-being, your life.

According to the latest theory of how the human mind works, proposed and researched by Dr. Karl H. Pribram, professor of neuropsychology at Stanford University, your mind "photographs" events in a unique way. Both a Neurological Surgeon and foremost researcher, his Holographic Brain Theory is one of the best working models for human brain science. It is this paradigm which sets the stage for understanding your own *"enchanted mind."*

Your mind is like a camera which takes pictures of events around you. These pictures are very special types of mental images of what you saw, heard, felt, smelled, and tasted at the time you took the picture. These are what we call our memories or thoughts and can be retrieved both consciously and unconsciously. The information contained in these pictures is activated by ATTENTION. Attention is the key; it is your power, your rudder, the control stick — the channel changer of your internal television set.

One of today's most amazing scientific theories is that these mental images are like **holograms**. Holograms are not two-dimensional pictures like the photos in your family albums or those in magazines. Holograms are three-dimensional pictures made with laser light. They are common items in our everyday life, appearing on charge cards, magazine covers, children's trading cards, and gift items in stores and novelty shops.

*

**Attention is the key;
it is your power, your rudder,
the control stick, the channel changer
of your internal television set.**

*

The two very interesting characteristics of holographic 3-D pictures are:

1) If you take a negative of a two-dimensional photograph, cut it up, and then project light through *any piece,* you will get only the part of the image contained in the piece you chose. The difference with a holographic plate is that if you smash it into a thousand pieces and then take any one piece, when put in front of a laser light, you get the whole picture. EVERY PART OF A HOLOGRAM CONTAINS THE ENTIRE IMAGE INFORMATION OF THE WHOLE.

2) By shifting the angle of the plate, a hologram can receive the information of thousands of pictures on the same plate. By changing the angle of the plate, the picture appears, disappears, and reappears.

These two main characteristics of holograms are what led Dr. Karl Pribram to propose the holographic brain theory. It explains some of the previously undefined mysteries of how the brain and mind work.

A movie camera takes twenty-four pictures per second in order to simulate the motion of "real life" on the screen of televisions and cinemas. The mind takes pictures in much the same way. The information in these pictures is then sorted (by deletions, distortions, and generalizations), stored in the brain, and activated by our **attention** which "triggers" the memory.

You can test this *information, storage,* and *retrieval* (I.S.R.) system of your *marvelous,* "enchanted mind" right now.

Have your biocomputer put a picture of a ball on the screen of your internal television set or, as they say, "in front of your mind's eye."

Good. There are thousands of pictures of balls you could have selected. Footballs, baseballs, soccer balls. Now put that aside and get a picture of a tree, any tree, from any time in your life.

Okay, now get a picture of your bedroom. Of your high school building. Of your favorite high school teacher. How about one of a teacher you didn't like? Now think of your grammar school. Can you see the front of the building? How about retrieving a picture of one of your elementary school friends? Now get a picture of your bedroom at that time.

By now you get the general idea. Your mind is a collection of **holographic pictures** of your past that can be retrieved. It is filled with archaic information. It isn't happening right now, though you can have an *instant replay* of the incident, or memory, you are retrieving. It is very similar to your family photo album at home.

The mind is an archival library. The pictures of the past have nothing to do with the current moment. However, they can impinge on the

*

The mind is an archival
library.
The pictures of the past
have nothing to do with
the current moment.
Life as we live it
is only in the NOW moment.

*

consciousness of the moment and change your feelings radically and almost instantly. They can even change the cells of your body.

As astounding as it may seem, these pictures control your health, relationships, prosperity, the depth of your spirituality and especially the level of your self-love and self-trust.

To illustrate this point, I would like you to go back into your memory bank and retrieve two incidents from your life. (It doesn't matter what age you were at the time.) You can keep your eyes open or closed, whichever way you are most comfortable visualizing.

1) **Pick out a memory picture of a time in your life in which you were very <u>sad or depressed</u>. Good. Put it aside for a moment.**

2) **Now pick out a memory picture of a very <u>happy or powerful time</u> in your life. Put that aside for a moment also.**

3) **Go back to step #1 to the very sad or depressing event. Sit in a comfortable position and run the movie of the incident in your mind's eye. Use your biocomputer screen. See what you saw then; hear the sounds, the voices (perhaps music); feel what you were feeling then; smell the smells (maybe something cooking or other pre-dominant odors) until you begin to feel**

sad or depressed somewhere in your body.

4) **After you have completed step #3, change your body posture. Get comfortable and run movie #2, the one of the happy or powerful time in your life — seeing, hearing, feeling, and smelling the sensations of that happy time, until you gradually feel happy or powerful somewhere in your body. Then open your eyes.**

You probably noticed, within a half-minute or less (sometimes it can take only seconds), you began to feel happy or depressed depending on which movie you were running. Whichever one you were **paying attention to**, the one on which you focused your "lens," was the one that influenced your feelings.

Isn't this an amazing phenomenon? Even if you are having a wonderful day and feeling good, if a depressing memory, for example, "comes into your head," it can make you feel awful, even though that particular thing is not happening *now* and you were previously in a good mood. You have experienced this many times in your day-to-day living.

Let's go a little further in our exploration of the "enchanted mind." Recent experiments at many universities have proven that not only can these holographic pictures influence or change your moods and feelings, but the picture you hold in front of your "mind's eye" can also influence your body, **right down to the cellular level**, and in an amazingly short period in time.

In *Omni* (Vol. 5, No. 5, Feb. '83), Marc McCutcheon reported on the results of research done at Pennsylvania State University. Penn State psychologist Howard Hall wanted to test the claim of some doctors that creative imagery helps in combating cancer. The white blood cells are the body's first line of defense against mutant cancer cells and other foreign invaders of the body. Dr. Hall took the white blood cell count of a number of cancer patients and then taught them self-hypnosis, which is basically the relaxing of the major muscle groups of the body. **Once the body is relaxed, the mind follows!**

Dr. Hall taught these patients relaxation techniques similar to the ones I will be describing in the next chapter. Then he asked the patients to imagine their white blood cells as powerful and hungry sharks eating up their cancer cells. Children were told to imagine "Pac Man" eating up the bad cells. An hour later, the white blood count was taken again. Hall instructed his subjects to practice the visualization exercise twice a day for a week. At the end of the week, the white blood count was again measured.

The results were startling. The white blood cell count went, on the average, from about 13,000 to slightly over 15,000 in the first hour, and a week

*

. . . not only can holographic
pictures influence or change your
moods and feelings,
but a picture you hold in front
of your "mind's eye"
can also influence your body,
right down to the cellular level . . .

*

later was nearly 19,000. Some did better than others, but the proof was there. "For some inexplicable reason," said Hall, "the mind can influence the body by changing the biochemistry of the blood."

There are many more examples of experiments like this; in fact, they have created a whole new field called psychoneuroimmunology (P.N.I.), the study of the effect of the controlled use of imagery on the cells and immune systems of the human body.

Many of us grew up with the idea of "mind over matter." At that time, it was just a theory, a philosophy for approaching your life. Now it is a scientific fact. Whatever image you pay attention to — especially when relaxed and focused — will have the capacity to change your feelings, your emotions and the very cells of your body. And in a very short time. Even using cartoon-like images of Pac Man eating up the bad cells can bring about profound changes in your immune system.

So imagine the impact you can have on your own "self-image," i.e., the picture you carry around of the person you think you are. That picture is not carried around for merely an hour or a week, but every day of your life. Whatever you focus on, *put your attention to,* regarding your self-picture, will have a life-altering effect on you.

POWER OF
THE SELF-IMAGE

Your self-image, the picture of yourself which you carry around consciously and subconsciously twenty-four hours a day, has a powerful influence on your weight, your health, your prosperity, your self-esteem, your emotions, your spiritual life, your relationships — the very heart and pulse of your life.

Continuing in the exploration of the nature of your mind, I would like you to make a collage picture of a "negative" you. Put together a composite of every negative thing anyone has ever said about you. You're too tall, too short, too lazy, a liar, fat, too skinny, whatever. Got it?

Now put the first picture aside. The second picture I'd like you to create is an entirely positive picture of yourself. Include every nice thing anyone has ever said about you or you have thought about yourself.

Once you've done that, split the screen of your internal television set, placing the two images side by side, and look at them. Which one is correct? Which picture can we consider to be a true self-image? Which makes you feel good when you look at it? Which doesn't?

Well, neither of the holograms is true or not true! What makes one or the other real or not real depends on which one **you pay attention to** and consider to be true. None of the information in our biocomputers is true, per se, without our consent. "Buying into it" and acting upon the information in the hologram activates it. This is the second principle of controlling our minds and becoming the captain of our own ship.

THE SPIRIT, THE MIND, AND THE BODY

For mastery of your personal biocomputer and shaping your own future, it is essential to understand not only the holographic nature of the mind and of your thoughts, but also *who you are* in relation to them.

All human beings are *spirits*. Many of us refer to this aspect of humanness as "soul." Allowing for the differences in religious upbringing, most of us acknowledge the existence of *spirituality*

in every human being. (In fact, most of us
acknowledge this in every living thing.)

For a human spirit to participate in life, it
requires a vehicle to transport it through our
material universe. Therefore, similar to purchasing
a movie ticket to get into the movies, each of us
must inhabit a physical *body*. We generally do not
pay attention to a being without one. What controls
this body and moves it through life is the *mind*,
through the use of mental pictures.

Perhaps a simple way to describe this inter-
connected triangle is to liken it to a stage play. *The
spirit* is the director. He controls the way the action
will go. His verbalizations of his view of the play is
the mind. The body is the actor. Upon receiving and
understanding the director's verbalizations, he, the
actor, physically performs the director's wishes.

Because the mind acts like a "switchboard," or
interpreter of the intention, it controls the outcome. Although the spirit is the director, it is
dependent on the mind to translate the message. If
you want to stand up, you first intend the action
and then picture yourself in action, and then (this
is greatly simplified) the body executes the thought-
picture-holographic program. Of course many of
the body's functions are on automatic, like the
beating of the heart or breathing, but even these
functions can be consciously controlled by the use
of imagery and creative visualizations.

Therefore, the pivotal point is the mind. And you, as the ultimate director, can make sure your mind correctly interprets your intent.

YOU ARE NOT YOUR MIND

"This way of understanding consciousness is used in Western philosophy almost exclusively to mean a reflexive sort of consciousness, self consciousness, or the distinction between self and other. This distinction is called 'intentionality' in philosophy and is based on the idea that *we can tell our own awareness from that which we are aware of.*" (emphasis added)

KARL PRIBRAM
The Holographic Hypothesis of Brain Function

"What we are looking for is what is looking."

ST. FRANCIS OF ASSISI, quoted by
Marilyn Ferguson in *The Aquarian Conspiracy*

For a moment, let's go back to the statement that may have surprised or confused you — you are not your mind or your thought pictures. When you understand this you will be able, in a few moments, to give yourself the great gift of personal freedom and peace of mind.

Close this book, hold it in your hand, and look at it. Make a mental image of it simply by paying attention to it. A holographic 3-D reproduction will automatically be photographed by your mind. Put the book aside, close your eyes, and retrieve the mental picture you just made. Who are *you* in relation to the picture of the book you just made?

Get a picture of a house out of your mental files. Look at it. Who are *you* in relation to the picture you are observing? Think about it before reading more.

That's right, you are the **looker**, the **observer**, the **witness**, the **viewer** of the picture in front of your mind's eye. If you *were* the thought picture, you wouldn't be able to see it, you would *be* it! Much the same way you can't see your eyes (unless, of course, you are in front of a mirror).

You are not any of the memories, thoughts, or holograms you've recorded, stored, and retrieved all your life. You decide whether or not to pay attention to the holographic thought pictures in your mental files. *You* have the choice. *You* call the picture up in order to "see" it on your internal television screen.

At times, a certain memory will "pop up" uninvited. You have a choice to either pay

*

You are not any of the memories,
thoughts, or holograms
you've recorded, stored,
and retrieved all your life.

*

attention to it and re-experience it, or to switch
your attention, like channels on a TV screen, to
some other holographic memory. You can also
make the choice to maintain your attention on the
present moment, thereby banishing the holographic
"intruder" back to its archival file.

You cannot hold two contradictory thoughts
in your conscious mind *at the same time*. It's one or
the other. Positive or negative. It's your choice.

ATTENTION:
What it is, What it does

"Attention is the process of consciousness
which gives rise to self-reflection."

KARL PRIBRAM

To a great degree, your perception creates your
reality. What you hear, see, and feel is the reality
you experience. Your attention is your life force. It
is much like a flashlight in a dark room. Whatever
you shine the light of your attention on enters your
awareness. You can choose to focus that attention
on something outside yourself or on your internal

screen — i.e., your archival holographic photo album. Your perceptions will be greatly affected by where you shine your flashlight. The Law of Attention is this:

Whatever You Focus Your Attention On Increases.

Think about the hose in the illustration below. The water in the hose is your consciousness and life force. Wherever you point the hose, the life-giving waters of your essence and consciousness follow, nurturing and making more real whatever has "captured" your attention. The diameter of the nozzle is your *focus* and controls the intensity and volume of life force consciousness being directed by your attention.

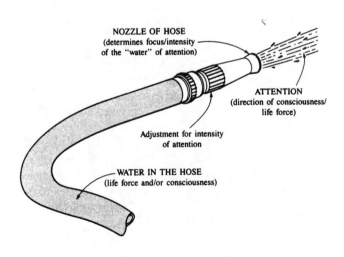

NOZZLE OF HOSE
(determines focus/intensity of the "water" of attention)

ATTENTION
(direction of consciousness/ life force)

Adjustment for intensity of attention

WATER IN THE HOSE
(life force and/or consciousness)

Figure 1. Directing attention.

**Whatever you focus
your attention on
increases.**

*

Attention is one of the aspects of your life which is within your control. If you had a glass of water (see Figure 2) would you say it was half empty or half full?

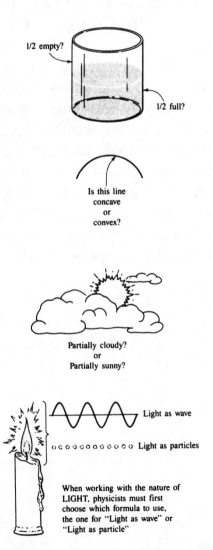

Figure 2. Alternatives in viewpoint.

Simplistic? Yes!

Profound? You bet!

Whatever viewpoint, attitude, or frame you use to approach a situation in your life will affect the situation. All stress management programs use this concept as their basis for technique development.

Look at the line drawn in an arc. Is it concave or convex? Continuing with the same theme, given a day with some sunshine, some clouds, would you label the weather partially cloudy or partially clear? As basic as these examples may seem, this technology of attention is in keeping with the latest scientific research on coping with stress and maintaining good physical and mental health. What matters is not *what* happens to us in life but what we *do* with what happens to us.

*

*

**What matters
is not <u>what</u> happens
to us in life
but what we <u>do</u>
with what happens to us.**

*

FRAMES AND REFRAMES:
Lemons and Lemonade

"An idea can galvanize the believer's entire being
even though it has no existence.
It colors our entire experience of material reality."

William James

What is the answer to the riddle of the ancient fable of *The Two Doors* told in the Preface?

THERE IS NO RIGHT ANSWER!

Your answer reflects whether or not you have a core belief that the universe is basically benevolent. It will give you an insight into your deepest belief concerning your feelings about the nature of life and your general attitude and beliefs.

What did you envision at the end of the story? When the wife chose a door, did the lover move quickly towards his fate, ultimately trusting her? Or did he hesitate, fearing trickery? What did he find? Did she send him to a brutal death, or did she allow him to live? Would he spend his remaining days with another woman or, perhaps, through a twist of fate, be reunited with her again as lovers?

Realize that *you* finish the tale and project your own beliefs onto the characters and their actions. Do you, and therefore the characters, operate with trust or distrust? Optimism or pessimism? Like the fable, you are the creator and editor of your *own* life story.

Your viewing point, your angle of perception, is called your **frame**. It is a map. It is *your* map of *your* life.

The frame you choose — what you put your attention on — affects your perceptions of reality.

Your capacity to **reframe** (changing the lens and direction of your attention) is under your control and affects your inner vision of reality. One of the benefits of learning to change your frame is that when frames are altered, they often result in new and sometimes amazing breakthroughs, both personal and global.

I am going to tell you a story about one famous man who reframed his way into history.

At thirty-one, he failed in his first business, and a year later, he was defeated in a legislative race. At thirty-four, he failed in his second business. Shortly after, the love of his life died, and at the age of thirty-five, he was so distraught he had a nervous breakdown. At thirty-eight, he lost another election and at forty-three, lost a congressional race. He lost two more congressional races at forty-six and forty-eight.

But he ran again when most would have given up.

When he was fifty-five, he lost a senatorial race and then, a year later, lost the race to become vice-president. Two years later, at age fifty-eight, he lost his second attempt at getting elected to the United States Senate. Finally, at age sixty, Abraham Lincoln ran for and became President of the United States, leading the country through one of the roughest eras in its history, the Civil War.

What would have happened if Lincoln had pointed his lens of attention to his failures and adopted a negative attitude towards life? What if he had given up? What if he had not reframed all his failures so that he looked at them with a new inner vision as times of learning and growing? Because he reframed his experiences, he was able to meet his great destiny.

This gift of reframing comes naturally to some people.

"When life hands you lemons, make lemonade." Many of us have heard that cliché, yet it is a powerful idea, i.e., reframing.

A famous anchorwoman on a major television network was interviewed about her success. She told the story of her first interview at a small midwestern TV station. She failed miserably. Her mother had driven her to the interview and waited outside. On the way home, in the midst of tears, the future successful anchorwoman complained to her mother, "I feel so humiliated. I feel like I've been beaten up, like they kicked me." Her mom turned to her and smiling, said, "Think of every kick as a boost and you'll have it made."

She never forgot her mom's brilliant reframe.

If you know your frames affect your world, then know also that you can select, change, and redesign all of your frames.

A famous general, not wanting to demoralize his troops during a losing battle instinctively removed the word "retreat" from his commands and instead said, "We are advancing in another direction." His capacity to reframe probably saved many of his troops.

The personal and societal perceptions which are *agreed upon* make up our frame of the world. And the frames you are willing to adopt and believe will totally color your world. In other words, if you are walking down a road at night, and all of a sudden you hear hoof beats, do you think of a zebra?

Probably not, and the reason you don't suspect a zebra is because your perception about your neighborhood is that it most likely does not contain zebras.

Or does it?

Perhaps posing this question to a member of an African tribe will result in a different answer.

We all have beliefs, ideas, and models of the way we think the world works or should work. It is our *favorite* way of viewing reality, though every personal and scientific breakthrough has come through reframing the way we see the world.

Remember the Wright brothers? They were laughed at for trying to build a heavier-than-air flying machine.

Dr. William Harvey was ridiculed by his medical colleagues for having the audacity to propose that blood flowed through the veins of the body.

Roger Bannister's peers told him the human heart would not survive running a mile under four minutes.

And everyone laughed at Ford's horseless carriage thinking it was "the work of the devil."

Each of these historical pioneers believed he could do something totally new, but he had to have the courage to continue despite society's ridicule and hostility. Now we hold them up as heroic models of the human spirit at its peak. Most of us would like to be like them.

Most often, however, people develop their beliefs and frames due to their perceptions, what they think they actually *see*.

Eskimos have over 70 different words for snow, far more than most other people. Eskimos are greatly affected by snow, so they need to create linguistic interpretations of their perceptions. It increases their ability to survive in their unique environment. Most of us have only a few words to describe snow due to our reduced need to express ourselves around that particular weather experience.

Linguistics follow on the heels of our need for added perceptions to our universe.

Sometimes people rigidly hold onto their frames, even in the face of proof to the contrary.

In the days of Christopher Columbus, people thought the world was flat because it *appeared* to be flat. Plus, everyone agreed it was. They thought Columbus a lunatic when he initially proposed that not only was the world round, but he was going to prove it by "going 'round the world." Today, the thought of the world as flat is ludicrous.

Perception is considered reality, especially when agreed upon by the majority.

Around the fifteenth century, the accepted map of the universe placed Earth at its center with all other heavenly bodies revolving around it. Why? Because when people looked up, they could *see* the sun revolving around the Earth. Copernicus, with his scientific research, reframed the whole story with proof that the earth revolves around the sun. He was accused of blasphemy and threatened with death for his views. Today, his perception of the cosmos is universally accepted.

You are in charge of your own destiny, no matter what anyone says to the contrary. The only limitations are the ones you impose on yourself. Your holographic beliefs are the "*tattoos on your soul.©*" When we are willing to challenge our own perceptions, and embrace new reframes, we open ourselves up to a wider and richer life.

*

You are in charge of
your destiny.
The only limitations are
the ones you impose
on yourself.

*

A simple axiom to remember is this: **The task of the subconscious is to continually prove you right.** It fulfills your self-prophecy.

Be careful what you tell it, especially in your internal definition of who you think you are. If you say you can, you can. Your subconscious will oblige you. If you say you can't, guess what? You can't. Your subconscious hears every word you say and will always do what is necessary to make *you see what you believe.* Thus the old frames of "I'll believe it when I see it" and "Seeing is believing" no longer apply. Now **believing is seeing.** It shapes the very nature of what we consider to be "real."

Internal programs of the biocomputer and its resulting *attitudes* often are solidified at critical times in a person's life. Some of these programs protect us from repeating hurtful actions. In a case of physical programming most infants learn not to touch fire by their parents repeating an earnest "no" combined with the actual experience of pain. Touching a flame profoundly stamps the psyche with the message that "fire is dangerous." It is how we learn.

In a case of emotional programming, a person might, after repeated experiences with hurtful romantic relationships, adopt the attitude that all relationships lead to emotional pain. That person may have imposed a self-inflicted life sentence of loneliness.

*

The task of the subconscious is to ...
fulfill your self-prophecy.

*

Sometimes our belief system protects us from both genuine and imagined harm, but each has an equal impact on one's life.

The American Heritage Dictionary of the English Language defines *attitude* as "... a manner of carrying oneself, indicative of a mood or condition ... a state of mind or feeling with regard to some matter ..."

Your attitude determines your altitude in life. It is a question of positioning your lens of perception, and deciding what you're going to focus on. The storms of life are ever-present with us. Think for a moment about your past. Perhaps you can even take a few extra minutes and run the movie of your entire life from your earliest memories up to the present moment.

As you probably realized, in your life there have always been some storms and some highlights.

Well, I have some good news about storms. Ship captains and pilots, trained in handling hurricanes and cyclones, head for *the eye of the storm.* Amazing as it might seem, in the middle of nature's violence is this area of complete calm, while all around it are dark clouds, torrential winds, heavy rains, and frightening waves.

You are the captain of your own ship, your own life. So the real questions become: Where do you want to place your ship? Where do you want to reside while making decisions or taking action?

Do you like being caught up in the storm and becoming what is called in the East "The Wave-

Tossed Man" or the "Drunken Monkey," being tossed here and there, up and down, by fate and circumstances? Or would you rather reside in the center of your cyclone of life, in the calm, peaceful "eye of the storm" as much as possible and handle things from there?

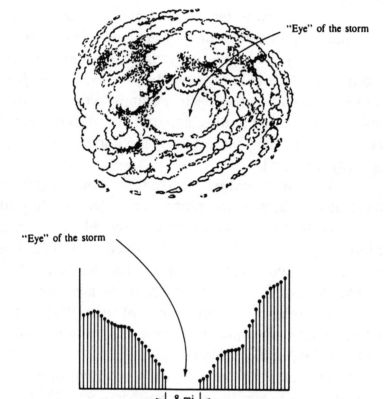

Computer printout,
Hurricane Gilbert 1988
SIDE VIEW

Figure 3. The calm in the eye of the storm.

Believe it or not, some people prefer the former, the roller coaster. And during certain periods of our life we may enjoy the dramatic thrill of such a ride. It remains a matter of personal choice.

*

Facing stark reality of life isn't always pleasant. It can sometimes be difficult and painful. But even in the worst of human circumstances, **we have the choice of viewpoint.** Even in circumstances where we don't feel any control over the events in our lives, our control can be exercised by our choice of both *perception and reaction* to the event. This applies to the entire spectrum from totally depressing to ecstatically happy events.

There are thousands of examples of this from personal life accounts of those who have faced tragedy and severe handicaps and excelled anyway. I am going to take the extreme example of what is one of the most physically, emotionally, and spiritually devastating situations in which human beings could have found themselves; one of the most anti-life environments mankind has ever created: *death camps.*

There have been a number of books describing personal accounts and research with survivors of the camps. One of the best books on the subject, written by Bruno Bettelheim, is *The Informed Heart*. As a psychiatrist in a death camp, he was fascinated by and studied the psyches of those who kept an open heart despite the unfathomable evil.

In *New Realities* magazine (July-August, 1988) Dr. Blair Justice of the University of Texas Health Science Center writes about the latest findings on how stress is handled by the *attitude* of the experience.

"The devastating effects of the Nazi concentration camps have been discussed for decades, but not much attention was given for a long time to the question, 'How did anyone keep going and survive such stress?' Psychiatrist Joel Dimsdale, then at Stanford University School of Medicine, located 19 such survivors in the San Francisco area who were in relatively good health, and he subsequently identified the survivors' beliefs and appraisals as the source of their successful coping methods. For instance, a number of the survivors learned to 'focus on the good' – which meant being thankful for getting through the food line without a beating, or appreciating the sunset against the distant fields.

The former captives also benefited from focusing on a purpose for survival. Some survived to be reunited with their families, others to bear witness to the world of the atrocities, still others to seek revenge. A number kept from being defeated by retaining a sense of mastery or autonomy over some corner of their lives. They persisted in observing Yom Kippur in the face of all odds. They learned to congratulate themselves on just staying alive in a place whose very purpose was to kill everyone.

. . . How aversive or damaging an event is depends on how we choose to take it. . . . All these studies suggest that hardship, difficulty, even danger cannot be equated with distress and increased risk of illness. The adversity we face does not determine our physical or psychological arousal, our health or disease. How we interpret the situation and cope with it is what counts."

The situation of stress can be imagined or real, the effect is the same. Perception is our reality, at least as far as the body is concerned, and I will be going into that in greater detail.

TWO SYSTEMS, ONE MIND

I would like to introduce you to **Lee Leftbrain** and **Robin Rightbrain**. They are two vice-presidents of your biocomputer "corporation," but you are the president and owner. Lee and Robin perform

*

Your holographic beliefs
are the tattoos
on your soul.

*

specific duties and functions. Although they have different "assignments," each carries them out in their own unique way. Both are essential for your life to be balanced.

Lee Leftbrain is the vice-president you have assigned to oversee the following:

1. logic
2. sequential planning
3. rational analysis and decision making
4. use of language, except for jokes, puns, and idioms (Robin's department)
5. mathematics
6. linear, intellectual, non-emotional thinking
7. investigation of the whole by breaking it up into parts (in computer terms, digitization)
8. quality control — the person on the end of the assembly line who is paid to find mistakes and flaws

Lee Leftbrain is the skeptic, the internal critic, the editor, who indulges in internal chatter. Lee uses approximately ten percent of the corporation's resources.

On the right hemisphere is **Robin Rightbrain**, in charge of:

1. feelings and emotions
2. unexplainable intuitions

3. dreams — including daydreams, flying dreams, precognitive dreams, lucid dreams, resolution dreams
4. the elusive quality known as charisma, attractiveness, "animal magnetism"
5. sexual energy (libido) and fantasies
6. personality
7. poetry and rich sensory descriptions of things
8. dance and rhythm
9. music
10. jokes, puns, and idioms
11. childlike or silly behavior
12. sudden personal insights, called the "Aha" experience
13. sudden scientific breakthroughs or problem solving, called the "Eureka" experience
14. sudden, non-logical compassion or sympathy
15. spiritual visions
16. praying
17. archetypes and metaphors
18. enthusiasm, passion
19. all parapsychological phenomena — including extra-sensory perception, out-of-body experiences, near-death experiences, psychokinesis, bi-location, psychic healing, etc.

Robin Rightbrain uses approximately ninety percent of the corporation's resources.

Now that you are more familiar with the functions of your two main employees in the bio-computer (mind), let's set up a little scenario. Imagine yourself sitting at the end of a long conference table. Last week you gave assignments to **Lee Leftbrain** and **Robin Rightbrain** to advise you about moving out of your present location and increasing your prosperity level. Should the move be to California or to Florida? They enter the room. Robin sits on your right, Lee on your left.

You ask Lee, who is full of nervous energy and dressed in a three-piece "power" suit with a tight collar, for his report and recommendations. Sitting with back straight up, military school style, Lee crisply opens his attaché case, takes out a thick, well-documented report with hundreds of computer printouts of cost analysis, and begins to read in a non-emotional, intellectual style. He addresses you in a formal manner. "The R.O.I. has a three percent override of cost through a ten-year depreciation of the Fowler curve's estimates of loss of capital in a three-year termed deficiency mechanism of yield over 789.3 for 4.2 years depending on the coefficient factor analysis code 5 . . . blah blah blah . . . ." When finished, with hands folded, Lee sits in a rigid posture.

Then you turn to your right and ask Robin for her report. Robin appears very relaxed, feet up on the conference table, wearing jeans, sneakers, and a loose-fitting shirt. "Well," Robin answers, "I really don't know. As far as California is concerned,

I understand the only culture they have is in yogurt." You both laugh. Lee does not. "Anyway, I just have a gut feeling that California would be the place to move to. Don't know why, it's just the way I feel. As a matter of fact, a few nights ago I had a dream that you were in California in a swimming pool full of hundred-dollar bills. You sure looked happy!"

So there you have it. Your two top vice-presidents have given you their reports. Who is right? Who makes the final decision? Yes, *you!*

As the president of this "corporation," you have the task of making the decisions. Oftentimes, we find ourselves experiencing two conflicting ideas, both of equal value, at the same time. Well, congratulations! You are extremely human!

My favorite definition of mental health is the capacity to hold two conflicting thoughts, emotions, ideas, or "pictures" in one's mind, at the same time, without going "crazy."

In addition to making a decision between two separate ideas, you have the added problem of not being able to trust your "bodily" informants. In many ways, your senses do not report to you in *totally* accurate ways. Your eyes, ears, taste, even smell can be fooled. Remember, we never truly experience things directly. Our mind interprets the signals coming in neurologically. It's second hand information. (If we did not filter the information, we would be overwhelmed neurologically. If things were not quickly prioritized by the body and mind, everything would come in from the environment with equal significance, and we would all live in total buzzing confusion.)

So what does all this mean? Essentially, you are accepting input all the time, both emotional and logical (i.e., Robin and Lee) and you are interpreting it constantly. *However*, it is also critical to know that you are an ever-changing being and all information that is "filed" is not necessarily cast in stone.

Dr. Elmer E. Green, a director in the research department of the Menninger Foundation, and a pioneer in biofeedback for voluntary control of internal states, says it best:

> "This left-right disparity is not limited in its effects to interhemispheric problems; it also can cause interpersonal trouble. For instance, my intensely left-brained father was often wrong, but for exactly correct reasons. And my intensely right-brained mother was often right, but for the wrong reasons. You can imagine how that worked . . . The functional parts of the nervous system are not 'hard wired,' or unchangeable. Because they are instead plastic, normally unconscious habits of body, emotions, and mind can be reprogrammed in brain structures by self-regulation training, plus your own volition."

In less scientific language, he is telling you that it is possible to change both conscious and unconscious parts of yourself. All it takes is desire and the self-programming techniques (covered in Part Two).

If we only make decisions based on our feelings, we will increase our chances of making a mistake. The same is true if we only use our mind without regard to what our feelings say. The best we can do is take in *all* the information about a given situation, weigh everything, and then come to a conclusion. It's a matter of balance.

SUMMARY OF PART ONE

1. You are a spirit in a body with a control system called the mind.
2. Your mind is like a biocomputer, an information storage and retrieval system.
3. Your mind takes pictures like a movie camera. They are a special type of picture called holograms.
4. Holograms are three-dimensional pictures that record everything you see, hear, feel, smell, and taste at the time of the memory.
5. Every part of a hologram contains the information of the whole. Any part, placed in front of a laser beam, will restore the whole.
6. Your mind is the control panel, or switchboard, between you, the spirit, and the body.
7. You are not your mind. You are the spirit viewing or looking at the information on your internal screen. If you were your mind, you wouldn't be able to see it.

8. The mind has two parts, two different lenses that focus on different information. One part (Lee) is analytical and rational, the other (Robin) is feeling and intuitive.

9. *Attention* is your power, the magic wand. Whatever memory or environmental stimulus you pay attention to increases. Whatever you pay attention to is what you are aware of, and becomes the reality for you no matter what is going on around you. Pay attention to the miracles already happening in your life, and you will feel blessed.

*

PART TWO

HARNESSING THE
POWER
OF RELAXED
VISUALIZATIONS

"Whatever you can do or dream you can do, begin it.
Boldness has genius, power and magic in it."

JOHANN WOLFGANG VON GOETHE

*

RELAXING YOUR WAY TO FULL POTENTIAL

Relaxation and visualization are natural skills you use every day, whether you realize it consciously or not. This combination has many names: creative visualization, daydreams, meditation, self-hypnosis, autogenic training, progressive relaxation, and even, in some cases, praying.

It has a profound effect upon our lives. It has an immediate, amazing effect on our body and our self-image and it has an astonishing effect upon the quality, the enjoyment, and the wonderful feeling of connectedness of the moment-to-moment experience of our lives. Now, in the 1990's, there have been major breakthroughs in understanding this process: scientific experiments have proven that the mental images we hold in our mind affect the body immediately, down to the cellular structure.

*

WHAT IS SELF-HYPNOSIS?

The term is derived from *Hypnos,* the name of the Greek god of sleep. *The word hypnosis is misleading and greatly misunderstood* because it has less to do with sleep than it does with relaxation and pleasant daydreams, which we all do naturally anyway.

Much of the credit for taking hypnosis out of the dark ages and restoring it to good standing within the medical community goes to noted psychiatrist Dr. Milton Erickson. Erickson was, to a great extent, responsible for the American Medical Association (A.M.A.) re-recognizing hypnosis as "a [valuable] therapeutic adjunct," especially in the treatment of stress related diseases.

In the early days of Western medicine, before modern anesthesia, hypnosis was used to perform thousands of operations and was the only anesthetic available other than alcohol or knocking someone unconscious. It still is used as the primary anesthetic in many operations today. Dr. Alexander Levitan, a cancer specialist at Unity Medical Center in Fridley, Minnesota, has used hypnosis in 21 major operations. "These included gallbladder removal, caesarean section, hysterectomy, and a four and a half hour operation in which a patient's jawbone was sawed apart. Only two had to be switched to regular anesthetic," reported *105 Magazine.*

In an article that appeared in *Esquire* magazine in January 1983, Thomas Morgan wrote about how he learned self-hypnosis to help him overcome a writing block.

Morgan wrote:

"How shall I describe self-hypnosis? I don't want to exaggerate. For one thing, *it is a temporary, self-managed altered state of consciousness that can make the resources of your brain and body and persona more responsive to your needs. Looked at another way, self-hypnosis is a natural phenomenon* that helps you follow your own suggestions, listen to your own admonitions, and submit to your own commands (Isn't that what you've always wanted to do?) just as the hypnotized subject in a one-to-one clinical session responds to the authority of a professional hypnotist during and after a trance. In self-hypnosis, you are *both* subject and hypnotist ... a technique that most people can learn in minutes and practice for a lifetime. ... Think of it! ... Self-hypnosis, folks, is cheap, healthy, painless, and useful, and it travels well through space and time. Moreover, it feels good.

In hypnosis, you are wide-awake but focused within yourself. It is not a waking dream – a *working* dream would be more like

it, a kind of businesslike hyper-consciousness
that lets you concentrate, really concentrate,
on a matter of importance without mumbo
jumbo at the beginning or rigmarole at the
end, and all under *your* control.

That is the point. Psychiatrists like to
describe the event in hypnosis as a trance. I
accept the word, but it is misleading, because
it describes the event only from the observer's
viewpoint. To most people, *trance* probably
suggests a spaced-out person dropping out or
away from reality, letting go, tending toward
zero – whereas to you, in your trance, inside
your head, you are in a vivid state of
concentrated awareness. You are still in the
real world working on a real problem. You
are in charge.

In general usage, the word *trance*
misses that sense of direction. It suggests *less*
control when, in your experience, it may mean
that *you have more command over your life
than ever before.* It can, I believe, connect
your unconscious to your problems. And if,
either within the trance or soon after, you find
new ideas, new combinations of old ideas,
unexpected twists of thought, or simply more
courage to go on, you will know hypnosis has
been working." (emphasis added)

In fewer words than Morgan, my definition
of self-hypnosis is "a pleasant and relaxed inter-
ruption of a person's normal hectic pace in order to
turn   the   healing   and   creative   problem-solving
aspects of *attention* inward, on one's self, before

engaging again in normal activities — refreshed, replenished, and renewed."

The principles in this book have started to become common knowledge. In the November 7, 1988, issue of *Newsweek*, the cover story was titled "Body and Soul." The subtitle read, "New discoveries linking the brain to the immune system suggest that state of mind can affect us right down to our cells," and it said:

". . . solid data connecting good thoughts to good health, or bad ones to falling ill, are still hard to come by. But lately, the doubts have begun to fade. The past ten years have witnessed an explosion of research findings suggesting that the mind and body act on each other in often remarkable ways . . . one study headed by psychologist Sandra Levy at the Pittsburgh Cancer Institute this year found that a factor called *"joy" – meaning mental resilience and vigor* – was the second strongest predictor of survival time for a group of patients with recurrent breast cancer. *. . . The immune system seems to behave almost as if it had a brain of its own . . .* [responding to] perceived social support and the way a patient coped with stress. *The idea that thinking well helps make you well is becoming a truism in American medicine, and mind-body clinics are now offering therapies for everything from headaches to cancer. . . .* Dr. Steven Locke, associate director of the Psychiatry Consultation Service at Boston's Beth Israel Hospital, calls the mind-body movement the *'third revolution' in Western medicine – ranking in alongside the advent of surgery and the discovery of penicillin.*

The least controversial of the new behavioral therapies are those aimed at problems like insomnia, migraine headaches, ulcers, colitis and high blood pressure. In the Mind-Body Clinic at Boston's New England Deaconess Hospital, Dr. Herbert Benson introduces people with such stress-related disorders to the 'relaxation response' – a serene state he describes as the physiological flip side to the 'fight or flight' response. Benson has his patients sit quietly, close their eyes and concentrate on a short word or phrase for a period of 10 to 20 minutes. *Those who perform this simple exercise regularly will become 'less angry, less depressed, less hostile, and less anxious.'* . . . *eighty percent of the patients were able to reduce either their blood pressure or their drug dosage.*

Mind-body therapies are also widely accepted as treatments for pain. Hypnosis, for example, is so potent a pain-killer that physicians have used it as a substitute for anesthesia in surgery. Just as a person reading a magazine may become oblivious to sensations in his back, the Stanford psychiatrist David Spiegal wrote last year, a patient in a hypnotic trance can become unaware of pain by focusing on some other sensation or imagining that the painful area has been made numb. A hypnotized patient may experience a surgeon's scalpel as a 'pencil being drawn lightly across his chest,' he says, 'and may remain free of pain even after emerging from the trance.'" (emphasis added)

If you cultivate your pessimism by visualizing negatives — failures, mistakes, faults — it will increase. Conversely, if you want to cultivate your optimism — talents, blessings, attributes — your visualizations of them will, indeed, improve your outlook. You might say this is all like Pollyanna, but science writer Daniel Goleman, in a 1987 *New York Times* article entitled "Research Affirms Power of Positive Thinking," says:

"Pollyanna was right, new research shows. *Optimism – at least reasonable optimism – can pay dividends as wide-ranging as health, longevity, job success and higher scores on achievement tests.*

The new research is an outgrowth of earlier work on the power of self-fulfilling prophecies. That early work concentrated largely on how individuals tend to conform to others' expectations of them, a phenomenon known as the 'Pygmalion effect.' If anything, researchers have found, the Pygmalion effect is more pervasive than has been thought. The new work looks at people's expectations about their own lives and finds that the power of expectations goes beyond mere achievement to visceral, emotional qualities.

'Our expectancies not only affect how we see reality but also affect reality itself,'

according to Edward E. Jones, a psychologist at Princeton University, who reviewed the research on expectancy in a recent issue of *Science*." (emphasis added)

Another example of the power of relaxed visualization is from Australian psychologist Alan Richardson. He wanted to see if physical skills could be improved with visualization practice, so he took three groups of basketball players and tested the ability of each group to make free throws. Each day he had **Group A** practice shooting free throws for twenty minutes. **Group B** was instructed not to practice. Now **Group C** was a different story. He had them spend twenty minutes a day visualizing themselves shooting perfect baskets.

As you have probably already guessed, the no-practice group, **Group B**, showed no improvement. **Group A** improved twenty-four percent. **Group C**, just through the power of visualization, improved twenty-three percent, almost as much as the group that practiced. Now you understand why American, Russian, and other Olympic teams have been teaching their athletes these methods.

Remember Roger Bannister? The so-called experts of the day believed it was impossible for a human being to run the mile in under four minutes. Bannister imagined he could, and he did! Of course, once other runners knew it was possible, they too began running the mile under four minutes.

Some of the most important research in the United States on using visualizations for peak performance in all areas of life — business, sports, and personal — is being conducted by Dr. Charles A. Garfield. Garfield was a team member of NASA's historic Apollo moon landing and is the president of the Performance Sciences Institute in Berkeley, California. He interviewed hundreds of professionals in the sports and business fields and asked them to describe the way they felt in a state of excellence. Then he compiled these reports into several hundred words.

The following is what they described when "on a roll":

"All at once it seems as though everything is working for me. There is no sense of needing to do anything. My actions unfold as they do in pleasant dreams, though my body may be putting out great efforts. I have no thoughts about what I should do or how I should do it. Everything is happening automatically, as though I have tuned myself in on a radio beam that directs my nervous system so that it works in synchronization with everything in and around me. I feel insulated from all distractions. Time disappears, and even though I know the speed of actions taking place around me, I feel I have all the time I need to respond accurately and well. I am so completely involved in the action that there is not even a question of confidence or the lack of it.

There are no issues such as worries about failure or feelings of fatigue. Even such feelings as momentary fear appear to serve me, changing automatically into positive forces. . . . I am acutely aware of colors, sounds, the presence of people around me, the feeling of being a source of power and energy in this moment in time. It is a trance-like state, and I feel . . . as though the usual barriers between me and the outside world have been pulled away, and I am completely at one with myself and the physical world with which I am interacting. It is a wonderful feeling, crisp, full of joy, more *real* than the everyday world . . ."

In his book, *Peak Performance, Mental Training Techniques of the World's Greatest Athletes,* Garfield states:

"Without a doubt, the most dramatic contribution to the advancement of goal-setting skills in recent years has been the Soviets' introduction of visualization. Use of this skill substantially increased the effectiveness of goal-setting, which up to then had been little more than a dull listing procedure. As used in goal-setting, visualization is a refinement of mental rehearsal techniques developed by the Russians. During mental rehearsal, athletes create mental images of the exact movements they want to emulate in their sport. *The Soviets found that mental images act as precursors in the process of generating neuromuscular impulses, which regulate and control physical movement. These images are holographic (three dimensional) and function primarily at the subliminal level . . .* The mental images act as three-dimensional blueprints for encoding the information required . . . In the process of goal-setting, we create detailed mental images of actions and desired outcomes . . . we enhance and accelerate our physical learning process by combining mental imagery and physical training." (emphasis added)

Soviet researchers in Milan, Italy, mentioned to Dr. Garfield a special government-funded, athletic program which integrated such a sophisticated combination of mental and physical training. They took world class athletes and put them into four separate groups with different training regimens. In **Group 1**, the athletes did only 100 percent physical training, while in **Group 2** they introduced the concept of visualization and had them work out 75 percent physically and 25 percent mentally. **Group 3** had equal physical and mental training. **Group 4** only trained physically 25 percent of the time while doing mental training the remaining 75 percent.

Which group do you think scored the best? If you guessed **Group 4**, you're right. It showed significantly greater improvement than **Group 3**, with **Groups 2** and **1** following in declining order.

Startling results, don't you think?

Dr. Michael Samuels, M.D., author of *Seeing With the Mind's Eye: The History, Techniques, and Uses of Visualization,* reports on the medical uses of the placebo effect. This phenomenon occurs when plain sugar pills or other non-pharmaceutical substances are prescribed for illness. Because the patient believes in the ritual of the prescription and has faith in Western medicine, cures take place with remarkable regularity. Dr. Samuels also used distilled water to cure peptic ulcers and colored dye to cure warts. Some experiments have shown sixty, seventy, even eighty percent cure rates for headaches, backaches, and other ailments, even though there was no reason why the sugar pills should have brought about this apparent cure.

It seems to follow, then, that **if a large percentage of people can heal themselves with a placebo, there must be, deep inside ourselves, some sort of switch we turn on that heals us.** No one has yet discovered what it is or where it is located, yet researchers know it is there, and are just now beginning to discover *how* it works. We really don't need to know *why* it works, what is important is to be able to activate the switch at will. For example, scientists still don't know exactly *why* electricity works. Theories differ depending on whom you ask. The important thing they know is *how* it works, thereby enabling us to put it to use.

Frankly, it doesn't matter whether everything we've reported so far is scientific fact, discovered by Nobel Prize-winning scientists or not. The only thing that really matters is, *does it work for you?*

After learning my easy methods of relaxing and visualizing, ask yourself these questions: Does the quality of my life improve? Do I have more love? Am I more relaxed and is there less stress? Better health? Do I have more fun and more enjoyment out of every minute of the day? Do I have more patience and understanding? Am I more productive?

If the answers are yes, the *why* is unnecessary.

REPROGRAMMING THE BIOCOMPUTER

Before I start talking about reprogramming old beliefs which keep you from operating at your best, let's pretend you already know how to do this, even if you can't put it into words. It is a natural, built-in tool of the mind and body. You may not have been told, but you were born with an internal "operator's manual," and it is in there for you to discover.

When you were born, your biocomputer was open to programming. If you are like most people, your mother was the first one to start giving you programs about how to live life, according to the information she had learned from her life experience. Maybe she programmed you to brush your teeth three times a day, wash behind the ears, always wear clean underwear in case you get into a car accident and have to go to the hospital, never have sex before marriage, etc. Well, sometime during adolescence, if not before, you consciously or subconsciously began to go through the holographic programs given to you by your mother, father, teachers, friends, and relatives. Some of the implanted programs or beliefs you kept, the others you somehow dewired. You still have the memories of the old programs, but somehow you defused their command value. You might still see your mother yelling at you to stay within the speed limit, but that doesn't necessarily keep you there. Other beliefs still have a hold on you, command over you, have mastered you.

So now you know *you already have the ability to program or deprogram any of your memories or belief systems,* even before I give you the latest formulas. You might ask why, if you already have that ability, you are not exercising it, but that is a question for another book.

First, to consciously reprogram or activate your highest potential, you need to get your mind into an alpha-theta state. There are four brain waves now known:

Delta — 0 to 4 cycles per second (cps), the slowest, during deep sleep

Theta — 4 to 8 cps, deep reverie, almost near sleep, but not fully sleeping

Alpha — 8 to 13 cps, relaxed yet aware, eyes open or closed

Beta — 13 to 26 cps, our normal waking, thinking, active state

Although it sounds scientific, your body is familiar with these states. I am going to give you techniques for entering these states at will, although you do so naturally every day. For example, when you are going to sleep at night and are not fully asleep but not fully awake, you are in alpha-theta. When you awaken in the morning, not asleep, nor yet fully awake or up and out of bed, you are in alpha-theta. Anytime you catch yourself daydreaming during the day, fantasizing, or fixating on an object like a flower, TV, or book, you are in that same magical brainwave state I call the "Z-Zone," also sometimes called self-hypnosis.

✳

HOW RELAXED
VISUALIZATIONS WORK

One of the reasons relaxed visualizations have such a powerful influence on our lives is because *the body doesn't know the difference between what is real or imagined.*

Think of that for a moment.

The body accepts both as the same and responds appropriately. Nightmares are a good example of what I am talking about. If we dream we are being chased by an angry bear, it makes no difference whether there really is one in our bedroom or whether we just imagined there is. Our body will react *as if* there is one there and will begin sweating. The heart will beat faster, blood vessels will contract, adrenaline and other biochemicals will enter the blood stream. The body will manifest all of the biophysical changes which accompany true fear, even if there isn't really a bear in the room.

Sex dreams are another example. Regardless of whether or not there really is another person lying beside us in bed, if we dream, imagine, or fantasize (all similar states of visualization), we will still experience all the feelings of sexual arousal, sometimes even climaxing in our dreams. Thoughts of your favorite dinner will cause your body to secrete digestive enzymes even if there is no food anywhere in the vicinity.

Now imagine a hot and humid summer day. See yourself arriving home and going into your kitchen to make yourself a tall glass of lemonade. Hear the ice cubes dropping into the glass, the gurgle of the water. Then you cut the lemon in half and squeeze the juice into the glass — just the right amount. And before you put the lemon down, you lick it. . . .

Well, how's your mouth? Did it pucker, salivate?

Although you may have reacted to this image automatically (unconsciously), it is the same body mechanism you are going to learn to control consciously for your own benefit. Remember, the reason self-hypnosis works is the body doesn't know the difference between what is real or imagined. Now that you understand this, you have a distinct advantage over others in controlling your life.

*

ENTERING THE Z-ZONE

Self-Hypnosis and
Relaxation Techniques

The first step in holographic self-hypnosis is to learn how to make the mind and body relaxed; then your subconscious is receptive to whatever positive holograms and visualizations you choose to use.

Dr. Karl Pribram, whom I mentioned earlier, is famous for his findings about how the mind forms pictures, how it influences thinking, and how our very neurology is affected by it. He says that when we imagine something with rich sensory details (what it looks like, what it sounds like, what one is feeling at the time, smelling, and tasting) it sets up a *neurological template, a set of instructions* to our mind and body. In a sense, *what we imagine or dream of becomes our rudder through life.*

Here are some easily learned techniques. Try them all, find the one you like the best, and practice it three times a day for a week or two. I suggest one of the three times be at night, as you are falling asleep, because this will help reinforce and deepen the technique. Perhaps the other two times could be mid-morning and mid-afternoon, when you need a "pick-me-up." Remember, it is not the length of time you practice, but the frequency. Five to seven minutes a session is adequate, though many people prefer more. Trust yourself!

You need only practice until you are able to reach the self-hypnosis state at will under any stressful situations, usually after about two weeks of practice. Then, as in learning to ride a bike, you won't have to practice any more; it will just come naturally whenever you need it.

Remember, since your body doesn't know the difference between what is real or imagined, if you visualize that you are on a beach, after a few minutes your neurological system begins to react as if you really were. So in a sense you are having what I call a mini-vacation. Bon voyage! Enjoy yourself!

*

BASIC RELAXATION AND VISUALIZATION TECHNIQUES

1) Take a Hot Bath

Hot baths quickly relax a person and promote good blood circulation. Lock the door and put a "Do Not Disturb" sign on it, or let the family know that you need thirty minutes of private time. You might buy yourself a bathtub shelf that goes across the width of the tub (a wide board will do) and gives you space for books, letter pad, diary, candles, and so on. Try massaging each part of your body starting with the feet, thanking them for functioning well. Move up each body part, taking your time, i.e., calves, thighs, etc. You'll be delightfully surprised at the immediate and long-term results.

2) Progressive Relaxation

This method was developed by Dr. Edmund Jacobson, an American physician, whose research into muscle physiology and relaxation gained him worldwide fame and set the groundwork for other psycho-therapeutic techniques, natural childbirth techniques, and new methods of treating tension-related diseases such as high blood pressure. Similar methods have been practiced for hundreds of years in yoga and other such disciplines. Here is the basic technique:

Sit down in a comfortable chair or lie down on a bed or couch. Again, try to take any precautions necessary to make sure *you are not disturbed.* You are going to progressively tense and relax your whole body, starting with your feet and then moving up your body through the major muscle groups. Take a deep breath, let it out, and tense your foot muscles slightly (not too much because feet and calves are prone to cramps) and hold for a count of three. Then relax. Tighten again, then relax. Do it a third time, then leave the foot relaxed and move up to the calf muscles. Tighten and relax three times, the third time leaving the calves relaxed at the end. Then, tensing and relaxing in sets of three, move up to the thighs, then the stomach muscles. Tighten your hands and arms three times each and then relax, letting them go limp on your armrest or thighs as you proceed to the neck and shoulder area. After that, tense your face and neck muscles as if you were playing with a child and making a monster face. This part of the progressive relaxation technique is often featured in men's and women's magazines as a way to keep the face young and wrinkle-free. Yoga has a similar exercise for the face and neck called the "Lion's Roar" for obvious reasons.

Now you have reached the last area, your eyes. You can start with them open or closed, depending on your personal preference. Tighten and relax the eyes three times and then, after the third and final time, leave the eyes relaxed. By that time, you will be in a relaxed state and can either listen to a self-hypnosis tape, have someone read to you in a slow, melodic voice, or do other favorite visualization techniques.

3) The One-Spot Technique

Sitting or prone, pick a spot in front of you and keep looking at it as you blink your eyes twelve times. Afterwards, when you close your eyelids, they will feel relaxed and tired. This relaxed sensation will spread through to the rest of your body in pleasant waves.

4) Mental Pictures of Relaxation

This technique may be the easiest of all. It works because you have previously conditioned yourself for relaxation by experiencing it some time in the past. In this technique all you do is get into a comfortable position and remember back to a time in your life when you felt safe, secure, calm, and relaxed. Holding the scene or object in your mind, using /all your senses — that is, what it looked like, what it sounded like, what it felt like or smelled like — will *automatically* relax the body. (Remember the reason hypnosis works is because the body doesn't know the difference between what is real or imagined.) It's called a *conditioned response*. You can use anything you have experienced, read, or seen in movies or on television, or even pictures from magazines. For instance, imagine yourself sitting by a stream on a perfect autumn afternoon and your eyes fall on a slowly descending leaf, going back and forth, back and forth.

5) Simple Breath Relaxation

As you begin to take slow, deep breaths, see yourself exhaling tension and stress. You can visualize this as a color that represents the negative for you. Then inhale calm and peace, seeing in the incoming air the color that represents relaxation and healing for you. Your favorite color is a good choice.

Another way, as you breathe easily and naturally, is to repeat over and over a word of your choice during the exhalation. Many people have found great success with the simple word *one*, because it has no distracting connotations. Other words commonly chosen are *relax*, *peace*, *love*, and *light*. If you have any distracting thoughts, just visualize them as a bubble on a stream of fast-moving clouds drifting by from your left to your right and out of sight, returning to your chosen word.

6) The Breathe Technique

Sit or lie down in a safe and comfortable place and arrange not to be disturbed. When you sit down, unbutton or untie anything that is tight or restrictive on your body. Close your eyes and concentrate on breathing in through your nose and out through your mouth. Feel the air coming in your nostrils and feel the air against your lips going out. Listen to the sound and the rhythm. Inhale slowly and deeply, pause a moment, then exhale slowly and completely, allowing your stomach to rise on the in-breath and fall on the out-breath as you breathe. In a few minutes you will feel more calm, comfortable, and relaxed, and your breathing will become slower and even.

7) The Eye Roll

This is one of my favorite (basic) techniques for self-hypnosis. While keeping your head level, you simply raise your eyes up and concentrate on the space between your eyebrows. After a few moments you will begin to feel a curious sensation somewhere in your body, usually in the stomach, and your eyes will quickly fatigue and close. Perhaps you'll feel a lightness, a general relaxing calm, a "floaty" feeling. Everyone is different. Get familiar about how *you* feel when you are in your alpha state of aware relaxation. This comes with a little practice. Be patient with yourself.

*

PARACHUTING
INTO PARADISE

**Various Deepening Techniques and the Creation
of an Internal Sanctuary or Visualization Room**

You might be interested in achieving even deeper states of relaxation and exploring the use of an internal private screening room for your visualizations. Let's first go into a few techniques to deepen your state of relaxation. The most commonly used is the "elevator technique." After you have achieved your normal depth of relaxation, you can deepen it easily by imagining that you are standing in front of an elevator, and the elevator door opens. You enter, the door closes, and you watch the numbers of the floors above the door lighting up as the elevator descends. Now you see that the number ten is lit up. Feel the elevator taking you down to deeper and deeper levels of comfort. Now you watch the number nine light up. You are deeper and even more relaxed than you already were. See the number eight light up. You are deeper still. Now seven. Then six. Deeper still. Five . . . four . . . three . . . two . . . one. You are now much more relaxed and comfortable, while your mind is more open and receptive.

If you don't like the image of the elevator, some people prefer using stairs, counting down from ten to one just as in the elevator technique. You could also see yourself *parachuting down into Paradise*, floating and counting from ten to one until you land ever so gently.

I always encourage people to make up their own techniques or images. Personalizing it seems to give it more power. None of the previous suggestions worked for a client of mine, and I suggested she come up with her own. After several days of experimenting she stumbled upon the technique of seeing herself rolling down a gentle hill through a magical hole in a hedge. It doesn't matter *why* that particular image worked for her, just as long as it worked.

After deepening your level of relaxation the next step is to create for yourself a private room, internal sanctuary, inner workshop, place of power, or personal laboratory. It doesn't really matter what you call it, or where you put it. Some people even choose to visualize it outdoors, / like a favorite private beach or a secluded mountain waterfall. You'll only need to do this once, and from then on, after using your deepening technique, you always return to this special space.

All that's required is that you return time and time again to the same place and that you have some sort of inner screen on which to watch your visualization, or a stage on which to see it being acted out. Make it as relaxed, comfortable, safe, and secure a setting as possible.

BASIC FUTURESHAPING PROCEDURE

Programming The Biocomputer By Making A Holographic Movie

Uses of the Basic Futureshaping Technique:

• Healing yourself • Healing others • Habit Control • Pain reduction • Creating an event • Increasing prosperity • Handling guilt and failure • Attracting the right people at the right time • Increasing self-love and self-trust • Changing circumstances • Enhancing skills • Accessing peak performance states • Changing another person's behavior without a direct confrontation • and much more. . . .

Now you are ready to visualize on the blank screen of your "internal television set." The basic technique is to create a movie for yourself. You are the star! You are the director!

When you are constructing the movie, pay attention to details! Fill the movie with rich sensory data. See, hear, smell, and feel yourself as healthy, attractive, confident, powerful, and successful. Imagine the scene, the event. Is it a sales presentation? A dinner party you throw for friends? An important public speaking engagement? Don't forget to include the other players — friends, peers, employees, bosses, even extras. It is not necessary to know *how* you will get what you are picturing, *just run the visual movie of already having what you desire.*

Once you've worked out all the details, begin to run the movie on your screen. You're going to watch it **three times. The first two times, watch it as** if you are the audience. See yourself and the other players. On the third and final time, act it out. Don't just watch it — *be in it.* Pay close attention to how you are standing, how you are feeling, how your voice is sounding, and how you are reacting to others. **Feel what it is like to have the thing you desire now.**

Once you have experienced the movie three times, reverse the deepening technique you have chosen.

Start counting slowly from one to ten, telling yourself that at ten your eyes will open and that in a few minutes you will feel refreshed, replenished, and rejuvenated, as if you had taken a three-hour nap. Using relaxation techniques to combat fatigue is one of the first applications I teach in executive stress management courses. Many participants recognize the techniques as similar to "a power nap." You will be amazed by the results.

You may wonder why it is highly effective to first **look** at yourself in your movie twice and then finally feel yourself being in it. Researchers have found actually *being in it* to have a more powerful effect on your neurology. For example, psychologists Georgia Nigro and Ulric Neisser of Cornell duplicated and expanded the experiments of Dr. Richardson's basketball free-throw research. They were interested in finding out which different types of visualization were most powerful. So they organized three groups of dart players. **Group A** was told not to practice. The people in **Group B** visualized themselves throwing the darts at a board as if they were actually at the line throwing. (They were looking out of their own eyes.) **Group C** was instructed to watch themselves as if in a movie or video, seeing themselves throwing. The results were that **Groups B** and **C** improved, while the no-practice group did not. The real surprise was that **Group B** showed twice the improvement of **Group C**. The placement of your *self* in the movie, or visualization, enhances its effects.

Most of all, remember that there is ultimately no "right way" to relax your body. It already knows how to do it. Just let it happen. There is no "correct" way to feel while it's happening. People experience a variety of sensations — everything from tingling, floating, radiating, and pulsing, to warmth, coolness, heaviness, and lightness in the limbs. Trust yourself and have *fun* playing with the various techniques.

KEEPING A PROGRAMMING JOURNAL

You might find it useful to keep a programming journal every time you "run a movie" in your biocomputer.

A good way to start the journal is with a "Personal Holographic Inventory" (P.H.I.). This inventory consists of writing three simple lists.

<u>List A</u>: **Things I like about myself physically**
When you make this list you need to be specific about your external features. Don't just write down that you like your face or legs. Start at the top and go down your body, part by part, i.e., hair, forehead, eyebrows, eyelashes, ears, mouth, etc.

<u>List B</u>: **Things I like about myself internally**
This list consists of internal personality traits you admire in yourself. Be specific. Do you like your sense of humor? Your sense of style? Your patience level? Compassion? Kindness? Courage? Loyalty? Your sense of responsibility? Prosperity level?

List C: Things I'd like to change (internally and externally)

Notice this is not a list of things you don't like about yourself. It's a list of things you want to program for change! For example: a flatter stomach, increasing your sense of humor, being more patient or compassionate, healing a tumor, etc. When you are just starting, it is more effective to begin with easier and simpler ideas. Let's say you want to run a biocomputer program to increase your sense of humor. Follow the steps of actually running the visualization — i.e., create the movie in your head, then enter it in your journal.

Write down "P" for program, "G" for goal, and "Viz" for the visualization — i.e., the movie you ran of *already having the thing or event you want*. Write out a short description of the movie.

Sample entries would look like this:

P.   –11/24/96   **G.** –increase my sense of humor
Viz.   –I ran a movie seeing myself at the office making my boss and colleagues laugh at the end of a meeting. Later that night, I was playing with my children and imitating Barney and making them laugh hysterically. My wife remarked how different I was and how enjoyable to have around.

P.   –11/26/96   **G.** –reduce the size of my tumor
Viz.   –I ran a movie seeing a pack of hungry, powerful wolves surrounding the tumor and viciously tearing it apart and devouring it.

One reason I suggest you track your programs in a journal is because *timing* is important. The bigger the change, the longer you need to receive the outcome. For example, losing 30 pounds generally takes longer than losing 5 pounds. Reducing a tumor will most often take longer than relieving the symptoms of a flu. If you've allowed an *appropriate* period of time to elapse, go back and reread the description of the movie you used for this change. Create a *different* movie, writing the new one in your journal, until you get what you want.

Whenever you get a wish fulfilled, mark the date received. As more and more of your visualizations come true you will gain confidence, power, and understanding of how *your* biocomputer works.

Remember, wishes DO come true, and the result may not turn out exactly the way you imagined! It's not always a matter of getting what you want but also of not getting what you don't want! Keep in mind, while you're wishing towards the future remember to count your blessings of the now.

SUMMARY OF PART TWO

1.   Relaxation and visualization are natural skills you use every day, whether you realize it consciously or not. This combination has been called many names:

creative visualizations, daydreams, meditation, self-hypnosis, autogenic training, progressive relaxation, and praying.

2. The use of self-guided imagery and visualizations can change the very cells of our bodies almost instantaneously.

3. Visualizations of movements or mental rehearsal of situations without physical practice are almost as effective as the actual actions.

4. Placebo experiments prove that *you* have the power to heal yourself in many cases.

5. The reason visualizations work is because the body doesn't know the difference between what is real and what is imagined.

6. Act as if something were true and, sooner or later, it becomes so.

7. Visualizations set up a blueprint, a *neurological template,* a program of instructions for the body to follow.

8. You already know how to program and deprogram your belief systems and behavioral patterns.

9. A relaxed body leads to a relaxed mind. A relaxed mind leads to a relaxed body.

10. You owe it to yourself to have one place in the whole universe that is yours and yours alone, a place of security and serenity that is internal and can never be taken away from you.

11. To bring about any event or change in your life, create and view a movie of yourself already having and enjoying it. Be, do, think, act, feel, dress, walk, talk, move, and gesticulate as if the change had already occurred and outside reality will, eventually, match your internal experience.

✳

BIBLIOGRAPHY

Bandler, Richard and John Grinder. 1982. *Reframing: Neuro-Linguistic Programming and the Transformation of Meaning.* Moab, UT: Real People Press.

Bandler, Richard. 1985. *Using Your Brain—For a Change.* Moab, UT: Real People Press.

Bennett, Hal Zina. 1986. *Inner Guides, Visions, Dreams, and Dr. Einstein.* Berkeley, CA: Celestial Arts.

Benson, M.D., Herbert. 1976. *The Relaxation Response.* NY: Wm. Morrow & Sons, Avon Books.

Caprio, M.D., Frank S. and Berger, Joseph R. 1963. *Helping Yourself with Self-Hypnosis.* NY: Prentice Hall.

Elman, Dave. 1983. *Hypnotherapy.* Glendale, CA: Westwood Publishing Co.

Epstein, M.D., Gerald. 1989. *Healing Visualizations: Creating Health Through Imagery.* NY: Bantam Books.

Garfield, Charles A. 1984. *Peak Performance: Mental Training Techniques of the World's Greatest Athletes.* NY: Warner Books.

Gawain, Shakti. 1979. *Creative Visualization.* New York: Bantam.

Hadley, Josie & Staudacher, Carol. 1987. *Hypnosis For Change.* NY: Ballantine.

Pribram, M.D., Karl. 1971. *Languages of the Brain: Experimental Paradoxes and Principles in Neuropsychology.* CA: Brooks / Cole Publishing Co.

Talbot, Michael. 1991. *The Holographic Universe.* NY: Harper Collins Publishing, Inc.

Wilber, Ken. 1985. *The Holographic Paradigm.* Boston, MA: Shambhala.

Wohlberg, Lewis R. 1945. *Hypnoanalysis.* NY: Grove Press.

RESOURCES

FUTURESHAPING TECHNOLOGIES, INC., is an organization that believes that the business community — because it already has a multi-national, global perspective — is in a unique position to spearhead the transformation of global markets. FTI delivers perspectives and techniques coming out of the latest research at major universities. It is dedicated to facilitating the business world's ability to provide peace and growth through prosperity and harmony. Communication is the thread from which the fabric of business is woven. Successful business executives understand how to effectively and efficiently influence others in the directions of growth. The successful secrets of these individuals are now available to be easily modeled and learned. After years of research, FTI has designed a series of seminars and products which give an individual the highly defined skills that quality communication requires:

• Telephone Skills Training
• Stress Management
• Communication Excellence
• Peak Performance in Sales
• The New Passion: Futureshaping Business
  In The Time Of Global Transition

And personal consultations in:
• Telephone Skills
• Motivation
• Conflict Resolution
• Goal Setting
• Personal Empowerment

FTI also offers audio and video training cassettes, other training products, and a free newsletter listing dates and locations of FTI presentations. If you are interested in further training for yourself or your business write (FTI, PO Box 489, Woodstock, NY 12498), fax (914-679-7759), or call (914-679-7655) for more information.

(ABOUT THE AUTHOR)

Richard A. Zarro, R.H., C.I., is a highly acknowledged pioneer and leader in the field of hypnosis. Over the last thirty years his work has been quoted in mainstream publications and in 1990, he was inducted into the International Hypnosis Hall of Fame. Recently his work was honored with the distinguished "Unlimited Spirit Award" by the International Association of Counselors and Therapists (IACT). As a certified instructor for IACT and NGH (National Guild of Hypnotists) he trains medical, clinical, and lay personnel in the art and science of hypnotherapy. Certified by the Society of Neuro-Linguistic Programming, Mr. Zarro has done extensive training with NLP's co-developer, the internationally acclaimed linguist Dr. John Grinder.

He is the founder and president of Futureshaping Technologies, Inc., a company which gives seminars to small businesses as well as Fortune 500 companies in the techniques of communication excellence, telephone skills, and peak performance states. His expertise and unique approach to critical business issues make him a much sought-after keynote speaker and seminar leader.

Because of his ability to speak on so many topics of public interest, Mr. Zarro is a frequent guest on radio and television shows. He is co-author of two books which have been translated into many languages: *The Phone Book,* selected to be in AT&T's phone center reference library, and *Changing Your Destiny.*

Mr. Zarro is an award-winning writer, poet, and artist and currently resides in Woodstock, New York.

HOLOGRAPHIC HYPNOSIS ©
CERTIFICATION

If you would like to be trained and certified by Richard A. Zarro, R.H., C.I. as a Holographic Hypnotherapist ©, and would like more information, please contact:

Futureshaping Technologies, Inc.
P.O. Box 489
Woodstock, NY 12498

Phone: **914-679-7655**
Fax: **914-679-7759**